Manners
of an
Astronaut

Shearsman Library Vol. 4

Gig Ryan

Manners of an
Astronaut

Shearsman Library

Second Edition. First U.K. publication
Published in the United Kingdom in 2018 by
The Shearsman Library
an imprint of Shearsman Books
50 Westons Hill Drive
Emersons Green
BRISTOL
BS16 7DF

Shearsman Books Ltd Registered Office
30–31 St. James Place, Mangotsfield, Bristol BS16 9JB
(this address not for correspondence)

www.shearsman.com

ISBN 978-1-84861-588-5

ACKNOWLEDGEMENTS
First published in 1984 by Hale & Iremonger, Sydney, NSW.

CONTENTS

In Blue Craft and Two Minds

1

You turn lesbian in the back-seat of the taxi,
his freak generosity nodding off,
wanting her tall mirror, her head ducks beneath a fan.
At 9 o'clock, being bored
ten times over isn't your idea
as the paralysed meal and her honesty stifles,
edging toward the easiest emotion.

You wake up in a splint of anger, illness, alcohol.
She fiddles with your paranoia till it floods.

2

She dismantles the flagon, it rocks like a ship
on the table.
He makes corrections, is one, and talks fast, apolitical.
She counts the keys and the clock.
His film of hands gesturing forever.

She wears the blind hammer on her chest,
pointing like Cuba at the door.
We have come, say the women,
to cry, and the poet, corny, American, obliges
with his accessible feelings,
his masculine one-way god
invokes Woman—the grave magic cut
where your tears go.

3

On a careless stair, the toy wedding veil.
Below, the endless mother
cleans up, forgives. She is open all hours
until you reek of sentiment like a poor book.
Her hand messes up his hair on television.

A car builds up in the drive
to a fast future where you pick bits out
like a sound-track. You force the clear screen
and want a new one, black and white, realistic.

4

Her head controls the room.
Outside, the second feature, its blue beckoning light cries
like someone else's kid can't,
goes into your mouth like a gas.

. . . .

In Hyde Park

As if a great sadness
longed in you. Not the small hand
or the desolate empire. Something is streaming
like light through a column of trees
into the brain's opening. That fountain
spills frozen in time, the people banging around, receding,
smile, walk, hold, regret.
That touch of a crowd you've embodied,
that shaky argument now constructs like a wonderful building
to prove a city there.
His mouth contracts like a birthday.

. . . .

Train

1

In the train's dressy dark, the smudges on his face
become a creed (Canadian in detail),
the cap swollen in his black central eye
is offering life in a minimal way.

The girl is careful, inconsiderate.
All night her plastic skill manipulates the machine.
She hums into range as sleep divides your head.

Think: down his damp length like an exercise yard,
your fateless likewise lust.
Think: such ashy clothes don't hurt
but the sole retreat gets harder.
This tank of wishing air has you in plural.

2

Her strict resuscitation, how his white mouth,
mending in the car, and the tiled room,
blocks your mouth like a plug.
He nods off in safety, and a kind of bliss.
Her black receding eye is flung at you
for a story. You shed like a friend.

In the car, his head goes down
like a window, and the gush of air, city, calculation
scatters, the poor quarters of another dream.

3

She's got enough equipment for life.
Her precaution rides down the train.
The water system flocks through walls
cooling and clearing. The moon you won't exchange
gives like a rope.

And he, poor thing, useless on his bad side,
is laid down, becomes her dead wood
and her rung. They keep them clean, she says,
like a set of awkward toys. You're fussy
about mountain air
and stay in bed, waiting for them to go away.

4

The irate garden is enough to make you pale.
English, he says, from another corner,
fanning the warm alien air, it's over to you.
You feel your face blacking out. Her huge heart,
urgent on the table, is telling something,
as a drug narrows the world.

These anarchists can't sing, their meticulous chaos
is narrowing a room, and his meditation
gets heavy—(that serene ideal isn't my idea).
He looks out from his worst defect, and waves.
With a bent book and a dreamy bible, you could
say it all backwards.

You want to die in the morning, the bed hurts,
and those voices belong to people who wait
in the kitchen with preparation, sadness, and things.

. . . .

Some Sunday

Yachts, and a lunch of phoney memories
keep the chemicals in business,
you reach down to second words, saying what's gone
like the leftovers he keeps greasing in the fridge.
The youngest is sick after. You can take just so much
of raw spinach, his subscribed brainwave
doesn't glow from here. To a cockroach
the room would look smaller, but to me
or your spontaneous friends there's never enough of it.

. . . .

The couple next to me think the photography's wonderful
and giggle through the words and the silence.
They eat the screen's colourful slab, and have found
something to do with the night. It stared like an awkward wall
in a luxury flat.

. . . .

An element of pity creeps into your wet relationship.
You kill yourself with laughing, the fake spot
where we met vanishes frankly.
We haven't died. You re-arrange the room,
but a trendy pointing bone
is in that laugh. The depressed American
wants quiet and protein.
Nothing is ever internal enough.

. . . .

His Cubist Drawings

You're shivering in the Cross, this mad bar,
with him all dreaming and response.
By the time you get home, you've lost the urge,
but think of him, he infiltrates your head even,
his cold bike taking off and your free hand dream.

Fun is enforced in a moment. It will wipe
most of you out, as you bring him round gradually,
being used to it. Leave your brain on that chair
and let Feelings just kick-start out of nothing.
Ennui is what the rich feel.

His cubist drawings are lying everywhere
between the dripping virgin and his male despair
that suffers, seeing nothing, in this neat artistic house.
Your sense of urgency would kill a car.

He borrows the mirror for hours to prove his clothes
are special. He shows you his delicate jewel.
You're supposed to sigh, and help him
with his coat, but talking about it makes me sick.
His pretty face swooning in the door is interruptive, male,
and the question, curious, oppressive. You will cut
that shiny ribbon to get out.

. . . .

A woman I love falls out of a strange shop
in the middle of nowhere. I want to be better.
Her fast mouth and her hand.
I'm about to have breakfast at 3 p.m.

on his money. I feel like a mess.
Her thin head turning and buried
is a good way to be.

. . . .

On the Liverpool By-Pass

1

On the Liverpool By-Pass you turn
just for the sake of the word.
Her friend and the anger
mashes on the road's quick curtain, as you drive illegally
in flaws, a slow drug shrinking the earth down
to one flawed, near emotion.

Call it yours, intrinsic in the sick moon.

2

At home, they account for it. A wide complex
fills her face in like an M.A. study,
the room vanishing with dialogue and correction.
His lost eye sinks through the floor
and she calls syllables.
Her black length in the narrow place
goes like a dip-stick to his mouth
and changes everything.

3

On television, the exploitation of children, love, etc.,
talking down to your thickening head, all glee
for some new make. The man wags his product
at the dreadful woman who spills over, bungling, unable, pretty.

4

The television's turned to a backdrop
while he haggles for attention like an ad.
His imperialism's not the latest, fitting a decade
once. A creek of air runs down your arm
as he mellows and lets the poor flaws free.

Go back to your room, the vivid cockroach doesn't hide
anymore. The walls are fresh with murder
and right aim. Read Samuel Beckett. Think of the future
where sleep comes over you like a gas-mask and doesn't kill.

. . . .

In the See-Through Wings

In this wasted room, your all-day friends sit it out,
the records, the drugs, the weak jokes,
and silence, cold and unsteady, keeps coming in.
They don't do anything. For them, coming home
is a holiday.

Sit on the floor, pure latency,
the television runs down like a person.
They made me listen, but my head was miles away.
He opens up his soul and picks bits out.
The dumb poet in a clever shot
drinks on the cover. I can't stand this music.
And when we're walking, I can't wait, turning back
to him, his gorgeous sensitive sunset.
He wants me to look at him looking at it.

Having seen god, they learn to breathe the right way.
Look, his soul squeaks. The room's medium poison
makes it easy. I don't know what to talk about
with you.

. . . .

Loose Red

1

She turns the conversation down to bite-size
and leaves through an evolving door,
taking care of her face like a contract
that it won't spoil. Profiles are serious,
they forget all about you and your thin planets.

Her painting is hieroglyphic
and when you've caught on, you can't stay
in a house of social dialogue. The shiny people
say things they've never said before.
A dull psychotic room fills with them.

. . . .

It comes to this, a stray kitchen
where you freeze to death. The nice warm people
talk to each other in a way that means exit.
A hanging tree shines in rain.
Wipe your face on that, run, as he delivers
a quiet premiss that might've killed thousands
and abolished you.

2

Mozart, opera, and science: I feel I'm a kid,
watching my father.
But it's Newtown. I left my father in Melbourne
with god. Here, there're only crazy people
who know what's good for you, men
who never make it, women who want to be loved.
I only like him as a person, she says coyly,
with that candid '72 sense of discovery.
You can date each attitude on your tour
of the past tense. It's what happens when you lose
the 'house of your dreams' in Surfers Paradise,
its view of processed water and the recent past
lift back into the envelope.
He stands in the door, fit for someone's crumby sentence,
wishing to be a tenor, or an athlete, even you.
Scrape the healthy muck from the fridge.
Everybody thrives on it. She wants space
and walks the beach all night.
I look at the stars tensing into position,
the muffled moon, a cloud's chemical slick
that won't be gone tomorrow.

. . . .

Your Night

I

It's alright for you, shaking this place out of a hat.
I don't feel like talking. Your steamy eyes
and these pranks in public aren't exactly cool.
Your beautiful face is lying on the table.
Is it really that bad? Tremor on *this* cone of heart
has learnt to shutup. As you wait till the freeway
to touch back. You're right. I want to build you into my wall
or talk to you somehow through an instrument.

2

He pulls friends out of a hat.
You remind me of the future.
but as for her cruel suggestions, No.
You can tell her. And your tin guitar
is like playing a factory. Get married. I don't care.
Do you think I like this sugar? Brilliant of you.

like last night when I thought I was in India or Heaven
spinning in your bed, in such an absence of murderers.

3

His reassurance record spins off,
its dark disc in this dark, glowing
with forgetfulness and past.
All authority is one. This dry flat of his
is hard on music.
You first. This book has swept me away.
Imagine being stuck in a lift.

4

Inside I feel terrible.
That park I left was worse than leaving you.
The blue pang of the road and my direction
have cut me up. It's pathetic to cry.
What do you want? To be nothing.

5

Her costume of flesh
is tucked into a chair. Strong imagination
and the pink globe of her face don't fly.
Swallow that, she doesn't, but canvas backs this hour
like a screen, you fold up the wine Patrick,
and look at this place.

It's the timing I can't suffer.
His wimpy revenge is there to be kissed.
At the corner, a man's sore face is trying to achieve something.
and the party is flat behind you, and in front the street
like a cord. But you wouldn't understand, weeds or anything
      don't grow
in this narcissist grey flute black night.

. . . .

Too Much

1

Like anyone else you're caught
towing someone around. A mild counterpart, or set
to get on. Easy on the door, and, you know,
gestures. Is this air graceful?
You could be a personal queen.
As you read the future like news, he means a lot.
And as you're broke, it's good.

Other people's mistakes are in books.
Yours, after all, aren't permanent. Oh expensive truth,
you'd make anyone sad. As I have carried things away
and left and cried. This is no darkness, just closer.
To act without confusion would mean something.
Whose heart? This rain, so rare and useful,
telling me.

2

Obscurity covers the coward of his brain.
This dense web was wrong.
Well, people go berserk when you say it.
So what? Since when were *you* grass?
His face looks private.
Some green lament is played, forgotten, sly,
and if his door hurt?
As if you'd worry too much.

. . . .

Eliminations

Neither ignorant nor wise
you approach life like Mastermind,
lose, like a soldier, you can;
that hurt note shines through even
this cake of air, accurate, heady.
Each day in your suede jacket
think of this,
your face just swimming,
the damp plank, orbit.

. . . .

Them, being special, cool, and 'liberated',
the lovers, meet,
to talk it over. The kids feel out of place,
this modern adult food won't go down well.

His good qualities can be seen from the island.
It's all lost time. Marry the wind, the table,
a way to be civil, as sun recedes like a tail-light
somewhere, you cumulative bastard.

. . . .

You wake up after the cold shower,
glad that he's gone, your man of the month
has just worn off. Now that's honest.
I didn't like the film, as you argue with the cops
and I lie.

Thick on the ground, the half-baked lunatics
manipulate a word. You've run out of listening
and want to kill, but instead a dream
hangs off like a limb.
Your mouth dislocates his face. I wish you were older.

I can't see anything in this go-slow drug.
Just lucky, I guess, holding his loose helmet,
looking at the architecture.

. . . .

Is that brief pain communication?
My silly soul drives badly round the concourse
back home, proving everybody wrong, why don't you
crawl our of that damned statue? I didn't mean it,
but there you are, all new and different.
Their stiff rhubarb rubs you up the wrong way, and feels good
like an electric blanket.
The motel purrs like a husband going out.

. . . .

Going Out

In the throes of blunt hate, the springy air
with him inside flips over backwards. That's education.
I don't want to go home, but he
doesn't listen. His brief novel rambling
like a soft grave.
He gets on my nerves.

. . . .

His coloured jokes and your black heart's cold murder
fumble for a cab. Too much. Leaping from the topic
like a boy, hysterical, smart. You should've lost that urge
and been pretty.

. . . .

The hollow gap gets still
and all the bright courting brain runs down
like a students' party.

That hollow kiss parts him
as, in a bad mirror, death. That's you,
feeling empty and invaded
in the stealing room.
With him around, nothing gets done.
The secret clock, his pestering,
sways.

. . . .

Tomorrow there's more deterioration
but this way things you can't imagine
like 'the gradual heart means it' come true.
That music reminds me of home, but in the room,
following it, there're only monsters
and a rough guess.

. . . .

Unable to love anyone, I turn back from the telephone box.

. . . .

I mean what *is* this, this mild skirmish, this lie

Your smart-arsed jokes stick around, but that's it.
What attitude now? Disdain and boredom are walking upstairs
in a flash. Look at my shoes. You cut the air up
with shadows. Your walk swaying and hard like a green lantern.
If I were Nietzsche, I wouldn't go home.
Can't you sing better?
But a song you've scattered anyway. It comes out with the machine,
the tacks of eyes, heads.
I mean, ghosts are one thing—murderers are something else.

My friend is chopping through depth, width, time.
Exhaustion, between planets, is O.K. really.
But I turn away from things to get rich, see, perhaps,
dreams are over it. Is night invalid?
Your grey skin falls over in my lap. Even you won't remain.

So a gun looks good overseas?
You live like a prince and hate everything. You'd get me
like a statement.
You're convinced about sex.
You rip into the joke like a crash.
Your charm has no heart in it.
Change before my eyes. And then your old voice
is torturing a speaker. I don't have to hang around.
As you jam up my eyes.

. . . .

Three things revolve on a brain's shed axle

1

Cut up the beans. Suddenly you feel shaky
and dim, as she bases you on something
and brings a whole new person out. Her excitable display
is almost ridiculous. As the conversation gets complex
you feel sick, but can't hide in a house that's uninhibited.
This anti-privacy swings like a sore axe.

2

On this side of the container terminals,
seagulls echo, and bats, nearly ordered, swoop.
His voice was a giveaway.
On the bus its broken triangle and her big flesh
cling against your arm like a different planet.

3

He endows a personality that fits
with saying nothing. His plastic face cycles and cringes.
Was it something you said? Those tricks aren't easy.
A car in orange flame looks remote,
as he rushes to the window like a victim, thinking of process,
    morality, exciting guilt.

. . . .

Going Backwards

Love has distracted me: its blue graph, erratic and complacent.
Here is his (pink) kiss, wet, nothing like water
and your amnesiac thigh.

. . . .

You talk about him like an object.
She points her dress around her on the floor
and sends a midget wave.
These animals on the wall are supposed to make you feel hunted
	and helpless.
She kneels down on the carpet and sponges away defence, the
	future, you.

. . . .

His junkie girlfriend has no heart,
just an operating table, well-lit, clinical.
She floods a vein with courage.
You fall over on the novel's bad English.
It's not enough, his all-day thought and a
good time. Was that him?
His face coming first.
the weird horse comes from the street; you've landed.
You can concentrate on the outskirts.

. . . .

His dreamt body is moody and ambivalent,
but that's just you. Your letters are essays,
the personal cinched to a question

as out of a comment, Schopenhauer is breathing
like a huge file room.

His love is full of significance,
as your heart is / less-than-ever.
Meaning waits at the beach for a good wave going somewhere.
You pick up the phone, just knowing it rings on Mars,
weighed down by conventional gravity, precognition, ace words.

. . . .

Her bad singing puts you off,
it makes life seem wet. She's no fun anymore,
her touched surface doing what you want
like a sensitive nut.

I look at his face. Inches are illegal, she says,
your wrists shrink, as the word, kilometre,
devours you. At work, the glowing window
represents thought. (Is that what?)
You act as if you didn't care, and then,
like a scientist, look

not exactly throwing streamers when love gets in.

. . . .

The Prospect of War

As a brain leaks out from its tiny emotional field,
it was nice of you to come, with your throttling hands
leaking out of affection.
This little place, response aligns
with what you thought you meant.
Good form here is lost like an old campaign.
What spinning trees beyond the drive
could wrong the face and hire the mouth
as this? What words? As your slack relativity
is keeping you alive. Who can live in the present, only?
But that's different. So is tomorrow.
The nervous bird is sticking up in the water.

Not frail stuff, his soul you had, but rock
and though your life in cool crumbs is falling everywhere,
you don't care. He fills it up like test-pattern. Not only America
will send the floor jumping, you with it,
but that kind of shock gets violent. I mean, would you sit back,
daunted, tell the agents to go home?
If only there were spheres still to think of
or a mat of ocean. That was your favourite, cut in half,
to remind the army they're mortal. Don't presume friendship
or pose with your money. He gets the river lashed
for being cruel. So in this modern well (or summit),
hands mean nothing, and wisecracks can explode later.
They've drawn a map of how the buildings and the population
could be hit. And the anti-death planes that can help you
right up to the last minute
are waiting on the outskirts of America.

. .. .

Morality Poems

1

Straw sticks out of the glove-box like a cut,
but they're your dreams. Go back to the country, Hiawatha.
You're lost here. The streets never get out
but go from one floor to the next
like a lift. Lack of pain and stress becomes
a broad welcoming committee. There's no arrow,
no river much either.

2

Their cruel and thoughtful lives are hiding something.
Like why is he holding your eyes now, steady,
a minimal table dying between you,
as her silly grasp and his idea of death
somehow make kisses out of gin.
This green wound his heart is ploughing under
is soft at first, but makes a shell of him.

3

We must be finished at all times.
We must throw away the idea of the finish, the end,
which is counter-productive.
We must work from the 'soul' outwards
though the 'soul' isn't here.
There are two ways of life for each person.
Only one is correct.
Light from the window reaches to the floor
and though in the corner, full of best intentions,
it's dark there, and behind your wish of eyes, darkness.

. . . .

Various Wars

(for Herodotus)

I want to fly to Egypt and look at it,
as we sit here forever arguing.
Why are good people so dull? But you wouldn't know,
obsessed with pulling tablecloths off quickly
and watching the remains as you are. This drug, luckily,
has narrowed me. Still, some dream-version of tonight
is loping, as a brain unweaves all over you.

And now, when you're talking, you're no problem.
Dots on the curtain become blank fire.
See, in my head, the hole they're shooting?
What happened to those buildings, that maze?
Does everything crumble, or hurt?

. . . .

So What

Separate things arc coming at you.
From the front room, cute jazz. Is it?
This slop hovering in the background like a new Hawaii,
and here, for instance, you're communicating things,
but in my head a last hour finds sense
and it becomes what I say it is.
Like his sadness makes you sad. Dumb to feel,
to wonder. If the night wasn't black, would you
with your turning heart, ever listen? Are you?
My dear invention, you can go now.
I've got this much, and your stunned key works.
His brain's small seeds pass for bright.
And downstairs still, music circulates.
I wish the night outside would come in.
Unload the door.
The sufferer may be crowned
but can you sleep like that, your eyes
jutting from door to stair to window,
waiting for that wrist of light to jam or just come home.

. . . .

Have to Go Now

This terror-sheet you hide from, these times
and the night settling for too much, have to go now
as, through the fence, stillness swoons inside you.
Another life gone, I've made the arrangement.
Sort through the pile you've been and come out, really,
wiped plank. But I saw leaves so bright
you're captured. Never is better.
Like a cloud you're not still, but perceived.
Clouds loom in your terrible head.

Rough break, some vanquished one is calling
from the sad arena, it's cracked onto you at last,
the movements to make. I often can't talk
especially when that face is shot into the room
and spreads. I can't. It's firstly stealing
and then ruler.

. . . .

Sum

Do I have to look at those sad eyes and feel them
pricking up and drilling, even from there. This muck
that gets between us. Though I wouldn't want to be you
if I thought about it. And it's not muck, anyway,
just inconvenient now to have to think, choose.
In another world, this gesture could be sweet
and you could just stand there, symbolic of things.
But meanwhile, people add things up
and the total is your head. My actions escape me.
I remember water shining like a cage, and not you so much.

. . . .

And Then What

Upstairs she gets obsessed with the idea of a biscuit.
While blowing under that tune
are chords that'd never occur to you
drifting and fitting.
And, in reverse, you're something. Reward and punishment
are waiting for you after death. Or are they?
Not everyone's like that, the worst most true
—you know, the sort of thoughts you dye to keep personal.

It's good not being alone here, this fake gaiety, the surface eden
they dream up. But then *you* become, well, stifling,
and I can't do things, though these wings are made of steel
they suddenly don't flap. Is it true you've become what you're
        supposed to be?

. . . .

Smile like a white ladder

Smile, like a white ladder. That's their famous trick.
But what could a mouth wring from you?
See where you've put that swab, that bag, their collection of eyes
is drying out. They are carving it out, them and their hard angels.
And you, still hanging around that swamp,
still dangerous in a way.
The liars have unprickled you.

Leave, must you, some river that was
and its trees tinkling like always drop yellow cares, flowers.
This good spot you dream, obviously,
and unwrap to some sucker like a bandage.
It's interesting how they hide things, they can do without logic
        even,
being clever in a bad light. How they invent numbers
to persuade. A block of solid stone killing you
and pulling up and telling you.

. . . .

All About It

I

It's supposed to send you to sleep,
but I'm awake. Satisfaction is a non-issue,
it teeters on the window's stringy ledge.
Its good counsel is divided between altruism and you.
Take half, oh puny fiction you write home.
Well, not there, telegram, I saw you blush and back out
where breath, exclaim, are words.
This stuff does nothing.
and the world looks up from its tube,
wanting to say, well, something.
A hand's hard trade is blanketing sorrow.
Just forget about it.
These brief and melting parents are liquid
in your loose heart, and thanks a million,
error, for that money, or pit without end. Have
faith is sending up some darkness
like a show. Don't mean it.
But Tuesday is rough.

2

He thinks silence is romantic, and now,
with a bit of you, he takes off.
Silence like a protection-racket. You give out
arrows at the dance. One for each bit,
one to keep you at least profoundly rotting.
Plain area sees things after days, the sky's white prescription
maiming you together, foot, wall, grip.
Feelings lose, you've got a better device,
whereas he's just everywhere. I don't want
these bits of you. His sheen of trauma
is absent for days. Sweet bridge—a vision,
smog.

3

The one who opens the door looks like a murderer.
As he shows you through each room's strange jarring backward
        language.
And out, in the concrete yard, a green mountain.
The tree in layers of being looked at looks bright
beyond itself. His mouth cuts in to pictures.
A small animal is fastened to his eyes.
and still, on the car's back window (trap), it's distraught.
Where is the magnet, green? This edge is soft
and flows in to a city. As I'm not earthed and float.
The benches are uneven. Just look:
soft colour splits. A rash of sky,
a failing sun. What else matters?

4

Take your time about it. She ambles.
I don't want a fight, and this wine is no tribute.
If you look at things properly, there's no change.
His face, her voice, wonky as they are, don't curdle.
She's wrong, but gives you money.
My boss gives me that generous-minded look.
I look at the Enlist Now! calendar. Maybe I will.
I gave him a hard time, but meaning interferes
with its deliberate gong. What are thoughts for?
He remembers his. and — Don't — goodness?

. . . .

How Long

1

His straight and yellow skin steers his parents' car.
I'm cold, but out of habit, look.
How long can you race the elevator up?
How long can you hold this stiff electric card
and change your mind?

2

Goodbye forever. Her brief life
I'm kicking out of. Well, let's face it.
I don't care about the china.
I don't care about your bitchy modern mother
or coffee. Besides, this flight
is better than you. Jealous table, split.
Your inch of fire is tedious.

3

Out in the streets, where grace is,
the pale machines are grinding faintly away.
Think of air.
His 'soulful' 'essence'. I dream of a fruitless orchard
with trees like grief descending.

. . . .

When You Feel

When you feel empty inside, idiots are better off
and sugar only kills you. I'm awake all night now
as if ghosts won't come. But now the strange stillness lit up
is worse. You can see the shimmering neurotic he's carting home,
his hand and her mouth a muffle of abstract ideas
fall away when they get closer.
The red Bradmill sign is burning like my heart.

. . . .

You make me want to die, oh crossed one.
The fit un-fit Australians tampering with the sun
easily laugh. Do you think I'm joking?
as your voice folds me up like origami
and puts me there for friends. You think sanity
is the quickest way out. But in my dreams
a woman swoons in blood and innocent men
deduce things, hesitate. Pick up your coloured blocks
and your masking tape. Some horrible liquid
is boiling in me. When glass breaks
in the road, a hundred sharp pieces
point up like a rough sea, and her jewelled voice
is singing.

. . ..

The Buddha Speaks

I have reached Nirvana. I have no desires.
I don't want to see you dead anymore, or alive.
This broad uninhabited plateau is heavenly, really.
I have eliminated the possibility of pain.
The slopes are crawling with pain.
Any movement, after all, is futile,
so I have cut down on aid generally
and talked myself out of violent feelings,
like a dense disciple not listening, or worse,
sweeping up everything you say and carefully
sweeping it into his mouth's dump, the words that is.
Those who ask are fools to begin with
so I let my wisdom come out, illustrating it
with little pictures, and my sayings touch those only
who are truly alert. The fools go away no wiser
with their lists and prayers. And my body sits quietly,
emptied of passions.

. . . .

Oh Blue Guitar

It's just hopeless. Their wired opinions make you fall flat.
They put on the wall a great frieze, which is life,
and you're in there, flat. And now like a cartoon,
you avoid them. Anything said is incriminating
as they examine the way you run upstairs, and discover you.
Her pokey eyes take away your clothes and leave wire.
He says this fit is neurotic. This fit that lasts for days
and makes things. Something is inadequate, to be so mad.
Try and get that room out of your mind, their pact,
their deception is making your pulse bang.
Just forget. O.K. His hands blench when he lies.
and their slow flesh is going down the chair
and her voice so bending it spills thickness
up the funnel of this house, my life,
and you can't stop feeling misspelt, the room's black obstacle.
And bad, like the way they hold swords
up in an arch for you to go down.
She, some other kiss, has somehow packed it in your hair,
      stopped sun.
His tender body is tied to the roof. Look at him soar, etc.
It's just. and you also get up and leave, transcend,
oh blue guitar.

. . . .

More

More brandy for this black day all round.
It started with that awful competition
of going blind and ends here
in a room full of resentment.
Not that brandy works exactly, but you
can crawl down a well and come out screaming.
Emotion is making everything disappear.
Everything is coming down to a drunk on the floor
and just a few simple words and a place
for my restless heart to lie down and love even.
In between, there was a street all blown and waiting,
a building you picked up, a car that got me,
and first, love's optical trick chucking ropes around
at the bus-stop. Your memories
also are blowing on the street, American and grey
and picked up also like someone else.
But here's this room back. Your oppression has no sex
but keeps hitting me. I know what it's like
when you want a fight. But I've got this stuff to drown in
come back come back love, I've forgotten today
and this room so bleak and magic.

. . . .

No

I

On my dead bed I think of you,
those priceless kisses and the argument.
True dream, we've messed things up.
Go, theoretically. As I turn away
from another set of eyes wishing I was dead
or better. You call this love?
this trance? these ghosts?
Love is like a cramp in the head.

2

Black speed circles and you fall down.
No-one can dance. As the bad music tramples out
and some are bored by lectures.
Have you noticed how an insult works?
To these people, it's like eyes are.
As they bat it and recoil.

Is it really conscience that makes you sick?
and does getting sick make you better?
People like god don't think so.
(He attacks his friends but we don't think it's funny.)

3

I have to leave your hands alone.
The effect is bad. As I go back like a baby
dreaming of nothing specific. Everything recently has been gentle.
But really, it's not good to be here making love
out of nothing. This red mark you did,
what does it mean?

. . . .

For the Flowers

He's been playing on a board for hours.
Look at his eyes, saying nothing.
Was that a word lodged in your throat somewhere?
Is it English? Whatever you've got
he wants to share. But I can't get through.
If I hear that riff again, I'll die.
There are, you'll admit, moments
when it's not just time barking at you
but something personal.

It's better when you don't talk.
It never was nice with us, but always some stiffness
crawling upstairs between us, and even now some new
unwanted person you've become
rocks in a faintly pink room,
rocking for the flowers and love's swiftness.

. . . .

Ode to My Car

At least the mechanics are honest.
My poor car, baby, you should be in England,
not here, withering. Though in the sun you can still,
not shine quite, but glow from within like a higher state.
Thin wheel of mine, last forever.
Or is that cliff immortal?

. . . .

Lines Written During a Period of Insanity

(I)

Regret in tears beside you bleeping every 5 minutes.
His mouth, in a permanent sense, seemed logical
when faith broke, but who can forget holes
and these sorrows pouring, or his extra eyes
not touching saintliness but coma. Your experiment works.
No blade is taken like a fridge
to your heart, but walls go away
or get sick. He wraps insight all round the year
then talks. So how can glass be loaded?
That diagram of friends includes a hospital, your head's hopeless
to be with, it feels angled and wrong.

You can sit up forever waiting to resemble 'true'.

(II)

This wedding's a dream, he will promise jewels, flesh,
but his heart like an angel cries on your yellow door
His eyes are about to go Russian, and love loyalty
and love her given heart, but your house diminishing
out of possible, and why are your yellow hands so naive
and the door meaningless?
Inside, music writhing out of place, why doesn't he scream
green letters out, like that poor seed once, broken, sent, your
        yellow soul
and her white dress, murder,
his lies singing himself out,
but his promise is vacant,
but then death

(III)

The gorgeous white piano is skidding through the room,
red jazz, and you, pink clarinet no-one asked,
not song, but a whole life, and before the stage,
a meal breaks, and some accessible hooligan
mislays this beauty
and now an inkling, suede notes lead in
to this sad set of keys,
and then his break like cars, green clarinet,
collide with me. Go East.
This club is made of flames. But I have watched the walls
lie down like a horizon, raft—your white hands
becoming sea, revolving clarinet, satellite and blue.
Piano beneath the veils.

(IV)

Remember Europe? Its dust also will lay you.
That record fumbles through scenery. At night on the plain
you walk through stars. And when you've left, your wine
upsets me. You have carried me away. I don't know you.
I don't know why you were making the floor dance.
Don't worry about the door. Don't bother me.
Remember where that faith went? Frail floating paper,
and the kiss you had, dawn was driving into my dreams
with your blue head. Caravan of death, I should let go.
There goes your soul, colt all over the mountains.
Green star, you're mine now.
And fizzing into my mouth, nervous circles sink
these bones of time. Like your face talks from lessons
and you didn't mean it.

(V)

Sweet hands, don't leave me
in this blindness. You get used to kissing
and liking everything. Regression isn't healthy.
This book has changed my life. Your house,
tortured like an albatross, calls to me
and the bad dream hammers birth and day
apart. I can't tell things, like the tree for instance,
its lock, its green vision riding from air.
White clouds in your room won't go.
The unbearable window keeps nothing, the sky's ghost
coincides with sadness. Only yesterday
I loved you. Today doesn't belong, and you've pressed back.
I'm soaring. Craft of forgetfulness.

(VI)

You make me travel like Egypt,
but I want to go home. Vain night, I've lost the river.
Your ark sinks, and it's through stars and cords of light,
no mystery, no horizon. The survey was wrong.
You balance on the floor, the cliff is aimless for me,
as tomorrow ticks upstairs. And for my sore eyes, you,
massive claustrophobia, manners of an astronaut.
It would be ridiculous to be happy.
I can't remember where I live.
And why 'rocks'? The sea's wrecked on them.

(VII)

That dripping note I left for you and the caving yellow house
I still stay in, though it's not there.
This man has spent hours on trains designed to hurt
and now, classic stoned, he chips the conversation up.
Without you, everything has the same silent texture.
Conversation doesn't grab me, and the door's plan of eyes
is throwing you away. There *is* no-one else.
The main street may as well be Holland,
the letters ageing in the box

(VIII)

The uncertain scary rock won't go away.
You think if you go out and practise talking,
it won't be there. But the bed is weighted with it
and the room makes verbs, and the face you drew in me,
not heavy, but constant, sings nonsense,
and these words disjoint. As if I couldn't follow
and this case of brains hits things
and goes out of place.

(IX)

while you, brave astronaut, don't talk to me.
Her monologue by now is desperate, and points faithfully
into the sky's pit, wandering with children,
and her pink eyes dream,
and her, melting into your dumb ears,
your stupid jacket lying on the couch till it drops.

. . . .

Manners of an Astronaut

1

Come out from the shower, singing and glorious.
Red light vanishing in the mauve trees.
Gladly enough, your head was only swimming, not president.
The lake with wrath is heavy
and reflections also have made it stop like a screen.
The lake through the white door isn't normal.

2

Bad heart, these 'feelings' fit easily
and move around inside like people at an airport.
The ones that broke out broke me.
Limp jar, you don't make sense, words rattle
in your heart, hit glue, fail.

3

With every vein you've got
worried, a hard clock taking away ghosts.
I heard the day start, not free at that stage
like when I listen to your hand.

The car and them pause.
Inside it they have harboured plots
that bury me with light. As this burden of electricity
gives a temple to my thoughts. You forget fast,
ex-one

4

Grains of madness fall into your bowl of cherishing.
Your heart, virgin and spent.
Cicadas siren in the backyard, can't scream over it
as he picks your equilibrium.
Even the fridge just about faints,
the light wobbling in your blue career.

5

It's not you chafing at my head,
these curled sheets rustling and how long
do these episodes flash for my life,
the pit of it, red, central.
Ash, you can come out.
I saw dawn.
and from the past like a jet, face it, were you.
Painful is the process of return.
Painful his evacuation.
And how sore can you get when you leave water
weighted in gravity, won't swim.

. . . .

From the Party

1

My friends camp in the mountains outside the city.
They're in love for the weekend, oh yellow rolling hair
of hers, in love with air for example
and not the plank of friendship.
At the party, balloons float outside music
and with them I swoon and feel ridiculous,
unable for 5 minutes to be anything.
He holds my balalaika and makes the room snow
and forget me. No-one hates you.
Strange party emotions are tossing like streamers
from his longing boat. White hills
foam in the distance. In the morning,
sex doesn't exist, and so you're dazzled wholly
by the flowers, your feet listening
and your brain like reeds.

2

His hands rocking and jammed on the black piano.
I no longer know if it's him, but just someone definitely
trying to drag me out of this. I know that some house
is waiting for me. I'll send blue telegrams
as thinking goes out of my head and picks up him
or someone. Her face in my room has this expression
because outside things concerning her go on.
And I'm here now because someone told me not to.
The sky is warning and sorry.
I've made your pink house green because I prefer it,
and fallen in love with a beam you shone through the door,
and your friends brought it to me and I fell in love with them
also for being true.

3

He sits in his room, wanting to have one good thought
before he dies. But thinking can be a mask,
as you give up trying to communicate.
The broken television and its white velocity
spinning out the hours.
I find it hard to believe rich film stars with causes
and can't any longer differentiate visitors.
Philosophy has taken a word to pieces
and now neutrality enters your mouth with it.
And death like a fur-trim on your coat
steals out of life. His physical word is turning
on the ceiling like a fan. Don't argue.
The room's ribs rubbing with etiquette.
How do you transmit lost?
The black lake is dreaming of poetry.

. . . .

Eliminations (II)

My body merging into its lost threads.
Playing cards bathed in drugs.
You go under the blue wave, as if hit,
sorrow opening its arms to some wet place,
count as if you are. Green sunset
undoes the room's atmosphere, and liftoff,
dust for hands and eyes for flesh,
you're losing. Grave tree that I have looked out of,
as from the building some emotional dumbo looks out at life.
A phone-call builds you up from scratch, gold voice slanting away.
His poor pretended mouth, his inside room
are living on the emotions.

. . . .

I run into people whose names I can't remember,
watching the blue hydrangeas.
The lost lane continues through the hill,
and speed has made me desperate
as my lost feet stumble on flat silence.
Sunset, I imagine, wouldn't make it good.
My feelings drop out in mid-air.
What's the use of drugs that make you similar?
People's faces are joining to form a pattern
of remembrance, and when they talk
it takes a face out of the file.
You want to marry him because he stares.

. . . .

A taint of insincerity is attached to everything you do,
its false voice smearing behind you like a tower.
False god, that makes these people ornaments.

His face is more sad,
and you stare in the street.
Foreign city rolling into our soft Earth.
Grey hallucinations of the sky detail and explode,
cut parts that you can look through.

Here, traffic spreads the street,
lights sink in the watery distance.
Look where we've come to, in blue space,
as sunset presses down.

. . . .

I repress his image, frightening my mind with nouns.
Is that the air-conditioning or the band?
Some stupid con act is behind me, his crippled mouth
like an aquarium—pack up and die.
Dancing with my friend, I become her, as we laugh
and fall for some sap. and on the stairs even
as if no-one had looked, his small and sudden eyes
are going through and my body means nothing like a picture
(it's mine), and how do you recognize things?

Her voice a chorus of angels.
I have cut his looks down. The white and open steps,
wild garden I can hide above and let words fuzz
between you so his eyes are returned. You will never feel
the sadness of his skin, his hopeful green verandah
and the sky intellectually miles away.
His circle we come off. Goodbye, poison that's lost in you.

. . . .

Blue Clouds

Blue clouds unfold the moon, its white reign
encasing you,
still fixed in the street like a god,
this uselessness. Between lost and seeing.
Wet eyes war speed.

The table circles with his bony friendship.
Advise the night. Red reasons shower the tree.
The curtain's black fish blows on my window.

. . . .

His face, green victim of the shadows,
drifting from the table and your arms twisting
air, talk of 3 a.m. and all the stars stick out.
This tray you've brought in, impossible, ajar,
and now his eyes are on it
and the house is sordid, and our relationship a mess
I want to cut off here, and think night might fall
into our eyes, the television like a crucifix,
and think, for example, he could answer
or change, the garden open like an aeroplane,
the white electric moon on grass, the wire,
and never end.

. . . .

But all dreaming is driven, the tree lapping on the fence,
and through flowers, the creaking house.
Silence and shadow are taking over me,
the grey street straightens the hill, the white sky,
steel cars, and at the end, grey constructed city
you've entered like a sheet of glass.
The colour of a flower can set your mind off.

. . . .

The vacuum of his face tortures me.
We'll never break through. His gorgeous eyes
should mean something, blank baby, what depths?

. . . .

Extortion and demand have lit the air between you
and you can look for so long,
but the wall and glass are waiting for your eyes
to come home. You become what you have to,
it's magic when you believe that his face, for example,
is designed from inside. Boredom is less torturous.
How your heart went bang. Look, you can dissolve it, him.

. . . .

Orbit

What's happened to your beautiful dress
your haircut disappearing in its concept
Without these things, you're a mess
I mean, the blind walls, the phoney dinner
Don't die on me I used to think you were perfect
And now in the ruined careful conversation
you're just a ghost and your eyes
carry the same green texture from glass to life to table
the same stare with a see-through word in front of it
fizzling like the cone between a film and its projection
Don't you realize I haven't slept for thirty-eight hours
and my face feels like a tight dress
and the room is meaningless and shatters with it
Calm with danger chipping out your 'soul', you thought lost,
your last love walking like a moon
and into the late kitchen.

. . . .

Advertisements

1

If you talk in statements, what do you expect?
I can't respond, humanly. Your university is the museum
you live for. Phone-calls don't matter.
I read your advertisement on the board
and prayed for rent. Tomorrow morning has no plan
but your chores press it like a knob.
How can I stand to watch as you circle the planet at last
and it doesn't move. Effort falls off you.
Here where the chair collapses and light doesn't work.
So what if the taxi-driver's gorgeous, his face
a sweet mixture of levels, the wrong road makes you think 'true',
and your stoned deadened brain is running into things, slowly.

2

As your eyes move from the television,
you see your legs have the bright scary look of reality.
In the room, someone breathes amongst live furniture.
Nothing's channelled beforehand. As you watch skin
and blood move spontaneously in the dense transparent air.
It's more fun being here really than on television.
They advertise Operation Noah and you just presume
an ark's being built.

This music lessens the suspense.
People narrate themselves. You don't have to be bald to be sinister.
The planes of his face turn around and look at me,
while there a coloured unreal sky quivers between trees
like a pond. Vague mountain, you don't care.
Months move in front of you.
I lie in bed terrified of Beethoven.

Tomorrow on the phone he's hassling like a kid.
Your bent time he'll come in like a parcel
and slow it. I mean, what's behind all this?
The nervous trees in their little surging plot don't mean the city.
You can have your suggestions. You're so mixed up.

. . . .

Let's Get Metaphysical

It's party-time in Darlinghurst, but he's sick of hairstyles
and those oracles of fun you give away like nuts.
Here it's raining in the kitchen, his black eyes glimpse virtue.
We hide friends under the bed
and can't get out of the room, stifling and affectionate.
How can you dance with your sprained ankle?
But you can't step back and separate the object from the process.
This thing is beyond love, beyond the brain's split.
The walls are singing with blue love
and the yellow sky dances with me
on days like this.

Enlightenment can't last, its silent smiling adventure.
I thought there was more to you.
The telephone is hot metaphysically
but his material presence is the limit.
What are you doing for lunch? I'm starting a charity until it stops
or else I'm giving it to you. The city like a map
isn't spontaneous. Listen to the lift's electric bell
as people freely pour out, and your free hour
wriggles to the window and jumps.
I don't like it when his body talks.

. . . .

Night

1

Your hand spirals away from your face
in frames of light
as you watch a mouth turning to concrete
and travel, stopped.
It's Lancelot's personality and not his looks.
She knows, as choice surrounds her like a sick lake,
and on the air weigh green and slumbering bodies, voices.

Don't you understand? Blue shape of ecstasy.
Why does the conversation have to fight?
It's unbelievable, pure mother,
the empty house is pouring like a state.

2

Soft cushion of memorized 'feelings' I take in my arms
and sleep in the long cramped room, you wave
to your head like a crowd and kiss goodbye the brilliant burning
    ideal flower.

3

Basically good people are at rest,
reality undoes its words.
The street and the park's loose objects fly,
form without light.
Words and days sleep.
and now, creased brain, context sheds from you
like water, and into the black falling air
sees stars. Forget about life.
The city's dotted glass reef.
Each floor, blind digits.

. . . .

Better Than You

You don't want a sister.
I'm not responsible to anyone.
It's no life waiting for a bridge.
It never pleased me anyway.
Usually, it takes the sky to make me better.
Don't describe your dead end.
Taking drugs can hurt.
Big deal. You're not like China.
You only all think the same.
Look at the cafe's interesting design.
You can tell everyone apart.
I saw one man on the rocky lake.
Now you're on land I don't talk to you.
Sun through the green window
puts god everywhere, even in your hopeless submarine.
He turns his qualities up and gets nowhere.
Your weaknesses are anxious.
Deep thoughts row me into walls
and sink me. But it's better than waiting for you, all walls.

. . . .

The New Morality

(for Dante)

She slams into a tirade of bourgeois justice
i.e., consensus truth. Responsible citizens warn you
for weeks ahead and pore over the map.
His looks beg for approval, but his head wants it.
Each cancels each. He doesn't rate.
She makes him say things he doesn't think
by saying things she doesn't think.
She calls on the good communal heart
she doesn't have, to exert power.
The new morality asks you to shutup.

. . . .

Her face flooded with cocaine in her triumphal bed.
Childhood didn't affect me.
Her body and her head agree. Pride leaves you out of Heaven.
After the desire for more (avarice) and the desire for repentance
have gone, you glide towards god. Singing is a journey.
When I reached the highest rank, I saw pettiness
had followed me. Prayers gleam on my head and blind me and god.
When I installed the swimming pool, I knew the Christians
        were right.

Fool, you're over-excitable. Toss your little learning deck out.
On the back, your heart's busted grip.
Mosquitoes dance on the wall. Those eyes you catch turn away.
He didn't mean to take my heart. His new car fills up
with gurgling orange air. I didn't see any personality
in your flat. My friends throw the phone across the room
after 3 days of speed, serapax, whiskey. I live only for the stars
and hear time. The art gallery listens to me.
We lie on the ground and hear the velvet trains.

Half Hill/Half…

1

Deep down of course, the group is gross.
Him being coy is just stupid
but, yeah, you can afford to be,
prying changing skin.
The bars of the street go to the new next place
where your yearly emotion won't come
and don't hail me like letters. You don't need to.
I mean, you've lined the walls and sucked drugs.
Nothing happens when I want you.
Three hours later, phone drama,
and next week, you're lying,
a bunch of success, green ally, that only gets you down

2

The world holds you in place like hairspray.
I walk home stoned, eating my favourite apple,
hearing birds fall out of trees,
super-conscious of walking.
How can you explain boredom in 10 minutes?
I get up from death. The drug's silent avalanche
and the world helping me forget.
What's wrong? ghost of separation
between thought and action.
If you complain here, you're talked out of history.
Suddenly you mean me. Lack of sleep has airbrushed your face.
Forget it, my brain catches up
and clinks callously inside.
This hill my sledge

So Far

Still
no sky can change the hotel's yellow lemon bedspread
and the exact chair breaking reality in half.
I don't want to touch it. My things ruin the room,
chucked in it.

In your hours without love I feel sick
except for good's bright coating heading for the cliff
I keep, except for longing tolled over your head
but don't expect telegrams. I dreamt of your gracious expression
making me feel bad. My craze is tinkling off so I do too.
The goods you relish die.
Secretly, the roads tear like cars. Doubt cuts you in pieces.
I can't face the racket of your friends,
anyway, life's perfect.

. . . .

Publisher's Note

Manners of an Astronaut was Gig Ryan's second collection, published in Sydney in 1984. I acquired my copy, now heavily foxed, on a visit to Australia towards the end of 1985. I knew little or nothing of Gig's work at the time, but her name came up in conversation with Peter Craven and Michael Heyward, who were then editors of the splendid magazine, *Scripsi*, in Melbourne – and have both since gone on to become significant figures on the Australian literary scene, as critic and publisher respectively. I had asked, as any literary visitor would do on a first visit to the country, as to whom I should be reading amongst the Australian poets, and was offered names that would now be no surprise: among others, John Tranter, Laurie Duggan, John Forbes, Pam Brown, Martin Johnston, and Gig herself, whose name came up as her chapbook, *The Last Interior*, had just appeared as a supplement to an issue of *Scripsi*. I've followed her work ever since, acquiring each Australian volume as it appeared, and seeing Bloodaxe produce a comprehensive *New & Selected Poems* back in 2012. (That book had previously been published in Sydney by Giramondo, in 2011.) I'd always had a hankering to see a Gig Ryan volume on the Shearsman list, and the Library gives me a chance to go back to that first discovery, a book which is not overly represented in the *New & Selected* volume, but which I think still stands up to closer examination more than 30 years later.

Tony Frazer
January 2018.

www.ingramcontent.com/pod-product-compliance
Lightning Source LLC
Chambersburg PA
CBHW020214090426
42734CB00008B/1069